101 CHRISTMAS RECIPE IDEAS

BARBOUR BOOKS

An Imprint of Barbour Publishing, Inc.

© 2002 by Barbour Publishing, Inc.

ISBN 1-58660-467-8

Cover image © Comstock

Scripture quotations are taken from the King James Version of the Bible.

Published by Barbour Books, an imprint of Barbour Publishing, Inc., P.O. Box 719, Uhrichsville, OH 44683
www.barbourbooks.com

 Member of the
Evangelical Christian
Publishers Association

Printed in the United States of America.
5 4 3 2 1

Contents

Introduction

It's Christmastime—time for shopping and caroling, church services and family gatherings. With all the demands of the holidays, how can you possibly create a delightful and delicious meal for your Christmas guests?

101 Christmas Recipe Ideas can help! From beverages and breads to side dishes and desserts, you'll find all kinds of ideas for your holiday celebrations. In each section of this book you'll find dishes that will complement each other and add *oohs* and *aahs* to your Christmas feast.

Dig in and see what creative, crowd-pleasing dishes you can create. With *101 Christmas Recipe Ideas,* your holiday meal is sure to be a winner!

101
Christmas Recipe Ideas

Beverages

Frosty Lime Punch

2 cans (6 ozs each)
frozen limeade
concentrate, thawed
3 c cold water
1 c lime sherbet

2 bottles (12 ozs
each) lemon-lime
carbonated
beverage, chilled

In a large punch bowl, mix limeade concentrate, cold water, and carbonated beverage. Spoon scoops of sherbet into bowl and serve immediately. Makes about 15 half-cup servings.

Christmas Punch

1 qt of grape juice
1 pt of lemon juice
1 bottle of
carbonated water
1 pt of ginger ale or
other sweet juice

1 pt of orange
juice
½ pt of
pineapple juice

Mix all ingredients and pour into a punch bowl with a block of ice. Sliced pineapples or oranges may be used as a garnish. Makes about 2 gallons of punch.

WASSAIL

1 gal apple cider
2 tsp whole allspice
2 tsp whole cloves
orange slices, studded
  with cloves

2 three-inch sticks
  cinnamon
⅔ c sugar

Combine all but orange slices in a kettle and bring to a boil. Reduce heat, cover, and simmer 20 minutes. Strain punch and pour into a heat-resistant punch bowl. Float orange slices in bowl. Makes about 32 half-cup servings.

CITRUS FIZZ

Very simple—yet refreshing!

6 c fresh orange or grapefruit juice, chilled
2 c club soda

Mix juice and soda in a glass pitcher. Stir briefly and serve immediately.

Sparkling Cranberry Punch

2 qts cranberry juice cocktail, chilled
1 can (6 ozs) frozen lemonade concentrate,
    thawed
1 qt sparkling water

Mix cranberry juice cocktail and lemonade concentrate in a large punch bowl. Just before serving, stir in chilled sparkling water. Makes 25 half-cup servings.

Orchard Fizz

10 sugar cubes
2 lemons, thinly sliced
¾ c lime juice
4⅓ c sparkling
    apple juice
mint sprigs

1 c soda water
    (club soda)
2 limes, thinly sliced
2 kiwi fruits, peeled
    and thinly sliced

Rub sugar cubes over lemons to remove zest, and place a cube in each glass. After squeezing, combine juice from lemons with lime juice, apple juice, and soda water. Float fruit slices and mint sprigs on top and serve in chilled glasses.

Eggnog

4 eggs, separated	1½ tsp vanilla
½ c sugar	⅛ tsp salt
2 c cold milk	¼ tsp nutmeg
1 c cold light cream	

Beat egg yolks together with ¼ cup sugar until thick. Gradually mix in milk, cream, vanilla, salt, and nutmeg, beating until frothy. Beat egg whites with remaining sugar until mixture forms soft peaks; then fold into egg yolk mixture. Cover and chill. Mix well before serving and sprinkle with nutmeg.

Hot Cran-Apple Cider

2 qts apple cider	4 three-inch sticks
1½ qts cranberry	cinnamon
juice cocktail	1½ tsp whole cloves
¼ c packed brown sugar,	1 lemon, thinly
if desired	sliced

Mix all ingredients together in a large kettle and bring to a boil. Reduce heat and simmer uncovered until flavors are blended, about 15 minutes. Remove cinnamon, cloves, and lemon slices. Serve fresh lemon slices in each cup if desired.

GINGER PUNCH

1 qt. water
1 c sugar
¾ c chopped Canton
   ginger

¼ c ginger syrup
1 c orange juice
¼ c lemon juice
1 qt seltzer water

Boil water, sugar, ginger, and ginger syrup for 20 minutes. Cool. Add fruit juices and seltzer water gradually.

MEXICAN ATOLE OR CHAMPURRADO
*A cornmeal brew drunk in Mexico
during the Christmas season.*

½ c masa flour*
2 c water
1 stick cinnamon
4 c milk

2 c brown sugar
3 ozs unsweetened
   chocolate

Stir together masa and water; add cinnamon and cook over low heat, stirring frequently until thick. Blend in milk, sugar, and chocolate, beating with a wire whisk until smooth. Cook slowly and bring to a boil once more and serve. Makes about 6 servings.

*(Mexican corn flour used for tamale dough and available packaged in Mexican specialty stores and some supermarkets)

101
Christmas Recipe Ideas

Appetizers

Parmesan Bread Sticks

1 loaf (1 lb) French bread
¾ c margarine or butter, melted
¼ c grated Parmesan cheese

Preheat oven to 425°. Cut bread loaf into 5 pieces, each about 4 inches long. Cut each piece lengthwise into 6 sticks. After brushing sides with melted margarine and sprinkling with Parmesan cheese, place sticks on ungreased jelly roll pan and bake about 8 minutes, or until golden. Makes about 30 bread sticks.

Cherry Tomato Blossoms

1 pt medium to large cherry tomatoes
   (about 24)
2 ozs cream cheese, cut into ½-inch cubes
   (about 24)

Placing tomatoes stem side down, cut each into fourths (*almost* through to bottom). Insert cheese cube in center of each tomato. Top with small parsley sprigs to garnish. Makes about 2 dozen appetizers.

Mushrooms Stuffed with Crab

24 medium mushrooms
   (about 1 lb)
3 tbsp butter or olive oil
1 shallot, minced
1 package (8 ozs)
   cream cheese, softened
1 can (6 ozs) crabmeat

1 tbsp lemon juice
1 tbsp minced
   parsley
½ tsp prepared
   white horseradish
¼ tsp salt
dash of cayenne

Remove and finely chop stems of mushrooms. Melt 1 tablespoon butter in skillet over medium heat. Add shallot and mushroom stems and cook about 3 minutes, or until mushroom liquid has evaporated. Pour mixture into a medium bowl and add cream cheese, crabmeat, lemon juice, parsley, horseradish, salt, and cayenne, blending well. Melt remaining butter in skillet over medium heat. Remove from heat and toss mushroom caps in skillet until well coated with butter. Place caps stem end up on a baking sheet and fill with 2 teaspoons crab mixture. Bake 10 minutes, or until filling is bubbly and mushrooms are tender.

• • •

*Christmas is more than a time of
festivities, family, and friends;
it is a season of
generosity, gladness, and gratitude.*

William Arthur Ward

Salmon Party Ball

1 package (8 ozs)
    cream cheese, softened
1 can (16 ozs) salmon,
    drained and flaked
1 tbsp finely chopped
    onion

1 tbsp lemon juice
¼ tsp liquid smoke
¼ tsp salt
⅓ c chopped nuts
¼ c snipped parsley

Mixing all ingredients except nuts and parsley, shape mixture into a ball. Cover and chill at least 8 hours. Coat ball with parsley and nut mixture.

Ginger Dip

½ c mayonnaise
½ c dairy sour cream
1 tbsp finely chopped
    onion
2 tbsp snipped parsley
2 tbsp finely chopped
    canned water chestnuts

1 tbsp finely
    chopped
    candied ginger
1 clove garlic,
    minced
1½ tsp soy sauce

Combine mayonnaise and sour cream. Stir in remaining ingredients; chill. Spread over crackers or use as chip dip.

Hot Sausage and Cheese Puffs

1 lb hot or sweet Italian sausage
1 lb sharp cheddar cheese, shredded
3 c biscuit baking mix
¾ c water

Cook sausage, breaking up with fork until no longer pink. Drain and cool completely. Combine cheese, sausage, baking mix, and water. Mix with fork until just blended. Roll into 1-inch balls and place on baking sheet. Bake at 400° for 12 to 15 minutes. Makes about 100 puffs.

Bacon Crispies

6 ozs finely chopped bacon
¾ c butter, softened
1½ c all-purpose flour
salt and pepper
½ c grated cheddar cheese

Heat oven to 325°. Beat butter, flour, salt, and pepper until smooth. Add grated cheese and ⅔ bacon and mix well. Drop by teaspoonfuls onto greased baking sheet, sprinkling with remaining bacon. Bake for 30 minutes or until lightly browned. Cool and store in airtight tin. Makes 28 to 30 appetizers.

Cucumbers Stuffed with Feta Cheese

2 medium English
(hothouse) cucumbers,
scrubbed
1 package (8 ozs)
cream cheese, softened

½ c crumbled
feta cheese
2 tbsp chopped
fresh dill or 2
tsp dried dill

Remove cucumber ends and cut in half lengthwise. Remove seeds from both halves with a melon baller and set aside. Blend cream cheese, feta cheese, and dill until well mixed. Spoon cheese mixture into each cucumber half and reassemble halves, pressing together gently. Wrap in plastic wrap and chill. Before serving, cut into ½-inch slices.

•   •   •

Let us remember that the Christmas heart is a giving heart, a wide open heart that thinks of others first. The birth of the baby Jesus stands as the most significant event in all history, because it has meant the pouring into a sick world of the healing medicine of love which has transformed all manner of hearts for almost two thousand years. . . . Underneath all the bulging bundles is this beating Christmas heart.

GEORGE MATTHEW ADAMS

FESTIVE NIBBLES

1 c all-purpose flour,
plus extra for dusting
1 tsp mustard powder
½ tsp salt
½ c butter, plus extra
for greasing
3 ozs cheddar cheese,
grated

pinch of cayenne
2 tbsp water
1 egg, beaten
poppy, sunflower,
or sesame seeds,
to decorate

Sift together flour, mustard powder, and salt. Cut butter into mixture until it resembles fine bread crumbs. Stir in the cheese and cayenne and sprinkle on the water. Add half the beaten egg, mix to a firm dough, and knead lightly until smooth. Roll out dough on a lightly floured board. Cut out desired shapes and place on a greased baking sheet, brushing tops with remaining egg. Sprinkle seeds over top to decorate and bake for 10 minutes.

• • •

*MAY you have the gladness of Christmas
which is hope;
The spirit of Christmas which is peace;
The heart of Christmas which is love.*

AVA V. HENDRICKS

Quick Brie en Croute

1 small garlic clove, crushed through a press	1 round loaf (1 to 1½ lbs) French or Italian bread
2 tbsp extra-virgin olive oil	1 wheel (8 ozs) of Brie
	1 tbsp minced parsley

Preheat oven to 350°. Stir garlic in olive oil and set aside. Slice and remove top third of bread loaf. Place cheese wheel on center of bread, tracing around and cutting down as deep as cheese is high (about 1 to 1½ inches), and remove center for cheese. Cut ½-inch slices around edges of bread, but do not cut through bottom of loaf. Brush garlic oil over cut surfaces of bread and sprinkle with parsley. Leaving rind, score top of cheese several times and insert into center of loaf. Wrap loosely in foil and place on a baking sheet. Bake about 30 minutes or until bread is lightly toasted and cheese begins to melt. When cool enough, guests may serve themselves by pulling off slices and spreading the melted cheese with a small knife. Serves 6 to 8.

CHICKEN BITES

4 chicken breasts,
   boned and skinned
1 c finely crushed
   round buttery crackers
   (about 24)
½ c grated Parmesan
   cheese
¼ c finely chopped
   walnuts

1 tsp dried thyme
   leaves
1 tsp dried basil
   leaves
½ tsp seasoned salt
¼ tsp pepper
½ c margarine or
   butter, melted

Place aluminum foil over 2 baking sheets. Cut chicken into 1-inch pieces. Combine cracker crumbs, Parmesan cheese, walnuts, thyme, basil, seasoned salt, and pepper. Heat oven to 400°. Dip chicken pieces into melted margarine, then into crumb mixture. Place chicken pieces on cookie sheets and bake uncovered for 20 to 25 minutes, or until golden brown. Makes about 6 dozen appetizers.

• • •

Christmas is
the day that holds all time together.

ALEXANDER SMITH

101
Christmas Recipe Ideas

Vegetables

Mixed Vegetable Medley

1 package (10 ozs)
   frozen peas
1 package (10 ozs)
   frozen green beans
1 package (10 ozs)
   frozen cauliflower
¾ c water

1 jar (2 ozs) sliced
   pimiento, drained
2 tbsp margarine
   or butter
½ tsp dried basil leaves
½ tsp salt
⅛ tsp pepper

Bring vegetables and water to a boil and reduce heat. Cover and cook over low heat about 7 minutes or until vegetables are tender. Drain and stir in remaining ingredients.

Steamed Spinach and Ginger

3 tbsp oil
1 finely chopped shallot
   or mild onion
2 crushed garlic cloves

1 tbsp grated fresh
   ginger
1½ lbs spinach
salt to taste

Warm the oil and simmer the onion, garlic, and ginger until soft. Raise the heat and add the spinach. Cook fast for 1 minute, stirring constantly. Add a pinch of salt, cover the pan, and steam for a few more minutes until tender.

Spinach-Cucumber Salad

8 ozs spinach, torn
  into bite-size pieces
2 medium cucumbers,
  thinly sliced
½ c vegetable oil

2 tbsp sugar
2 tbsp vinegar
2 tsp soy sauce
½ tsp dry mustard
¼ tsp garlic powder

Put spinach and cucumbers in tightly closed plastic bag, refrigerate up to 24 hours. Mix remaining ingredients in a tightly covered jar and refrigerate. Before serving, shake dressing and toss with spinach and cucumbers.

Brussels Sprouts and Chestnuts

2¼ lbs Brussels sprouts
1 can (8 ozs) chestnuts
2 c chicken stock,
  rinsed and drained

2 tbsp butter
salt (optional)
freshly ground
  black pepper

Cut a slice from base of each Brussels sprout and tear off outer leaves. Bring chicken stock to a boil in pan and place steamer containing sprouts over pan and cover. Steam for 6 to 8 minutes until sprouts are tender. Stir sprouts and chestnuts in melted butter over medium heat for 2 to 3 minutes. Transfer to a warm serving dish and season with pepper. Serves 8.

Antipasto Toss

1 can (15 ozs) garbanzo beans, drained
1 jar (about 6 ozs) marinated artichoke hearts
½ c pitted ripe olives, cut into halves
½ c herb-and-garlic or Italian salad dressing
2 bunches romaine lettuce, torn into
    bite-size pieces
1 bunch leaf lettuce, torn into bite-size pieces
½ c sliced pepperoni, if desired
freshly ground pepper

Mix beans, artichoke hearts (with liquid), olives, and salad dressing. Cover and refrigerate. Toss with remaining ingredients just before serving.

Green Peas with Celery and Onion

2 packages (10 ozs each)   3 tbsp margarine or
    frozen peas   butter, softened
½ c sliced celery   ¼ tsp salt
1 small onion, thinly sliced

Following directions on package for peas, cook celery, onion, and peas; drain. Stir in margarine and salt.

Mixed Green Salad
with Parmesan Walnuts

1 small head lettuce
1 small bunch leaf lettuce
½ small bunch endive
4 ozs spinach

¼ c oil and vinegar
   salad dressing
Parmesan Walnuts
   (see recipe below)

Tear salad greens into bite-size pieces and toss with salad dressing until well coated. Stir in ½ to 1 cup Parmesan Walnuts.

Parmesan Walnuts

1 tbsp margarine or butter
⅛ tsp hickory smoked salt
⅛ tsp salt

1 c walnuts
2 tbsp grated
   Parmesan cheese

Place margarine, hickory salt, and salt in a 9x9x2-inch baking pan and heat at 350° for 2 to 3 minutes, or until bubbly. Stir in walnuts and heat 5 minutes. Add Parmesan cheese and stir; return to oven for 3 to 5 minutes until cheese is lightly browned.

Asparagus with Pimiento

2 packages (10 ozs each)
   frozen asparagus spears
lemon juice

margarine or butter
pimiento strips

Cook frozen asparagus spears according to package directions and drain. Drizzle with lemon juice and melted butter or margarine. Garnish with pimiento strips.

Green Bean Buffet Salad

3 lbs fresh green beans
½ medium sweet onion
   (yellow, white, or
   purple), sliced paper
   thin (optional)

balsamic vinaigrette
1 jar (7 ozs) roasted
   red peppers
½ c oil-cured black
   olives, pitted

Snap off bean ends, and if large, cut in half. Add beans to boiling salt water. When water returns to a rolling boil, cook 3 to 5 minutes, until crisp-tender. Drain in colander and rinse under cold running water. Drain liquid from roasted peppers and cut into ¼-inch strips. Toss lightly with green beans and onion slices. Prior to serving, pour vinaigrette over vegetables and toss until well coated. Scatter olives over top.

Caramelized Carrots and Pearl Onions

1½ lbs carrots, peeled and cut into thin rings

8 ozs pearl onions, peeled

3 tbsp butter

6 tbsp chicken stock

1 tbsp sugar

freshly ground black pepper

salt

Bring carrots and onions to a boil in a pan of salted water over high heat. Boil for 1 minute and drain. Return to pan, add butter, chicken stock, and sugar and bring to a boil over medium heat, stirring occasionally. Cover and simmer over low heat until all liquid has been absorbed into vegetables and they are glossy and dry. Season with salt and pepper, and serve.

• • •

And in the sixth month the angel Gabriel was sent from God unto a city of Galilee, named Nazareth, to a virgin espoused to a man whose name was Joseph, of the house of David; and the virgin's name was Mary.

And the angel came in unto her, and said, Hail, thou that art highly favoured, the Lord is with thee: blessed art thou among women. And when she saw him, she was troubled at his saying, and cast in her mind what manner of salutation this should be.

And the angel said unto her, Fear not, Mary: for thou hast found favour with God. And, behold, thou shalt conceive in thy womb, and bring forth a son, and shalt call his name JESUS. He shall be great, and shall be called the Son of the Highest. LUKE 1:26–32

Golden Squash Casserole

6 c cubed, pared
   Hubbard squash*
	1 medium onion,
	   finely chopped

1 c dairy sour cream	1 tsp salt
2 tbsp margarine or butter	¼ tsp pepper

Place 1 inch of salted water in pan and bring to a boil. Add squash, cover, and return to a boil. Cook 15 to 20 minutes or until tender; drain. After mashing squash, stir in remaining ingredients. Pour into ungreased, 1-quart casserole. Bake uncovered at 325° for 35 to 45 minutes or until hot.

*2 packages (12 ounces each) frozen cooked squash, thawed, can be substituted for the cooked fresh squash.

• • •

Somehow, *not only for Christmas,*
But all the long year through,
The joy that you give to others,
Is the joy that comes back to you.
And the more you spend in blessing,
The poor and lonely and sad,
The more of your heart's possessing,
Returns to you glad.

JOHN GREENLEAF WHITTIER

101
Christmas Recipe Ideas

Breads

CRANBERRY-ORANGE NUT BREAD

2 c all-purpose flour	1 tbsp grated
¾ c sugar	orange peel
1½ tsp baking powder	¾ c orange juice
¾ tsp salt	1 egg
½ tsp baking soda	1 c cranberries,
¼ c margarine or butter,	chopped
softened	½ c chopped nuts

Heat oven to 350°. Grease bottom only of 9x5x3-inch loaf pan. Combine flour, sugar, baking powder, salt, and baking soda; cut in margarine until crumbly. Add orange peel, orange juice, and egg, and stir just until moistened. Mix in cranberries and nuts. Pour into prepared pan and bake 55 to 65 minutes, or until wooden toothpick inserted in center comes out clean. Cool completely before slicing.

• • •

Silent night, holy night,
Son of God, love's pure light;
Radiant beams from Thy holy face
With the dawn of redeeming grace,
Jesus, Lord, at Thy birth,
Jesus, Lord, at Thy birth.

JOSEF MOHR,
"Silent Night"

Potato Rosemary Bread

2 medium baking potatoes,
  peeled and cut into
  1-inch chunks
½ tsp minced rosemary
2 c flour

1 envelope (½ oz)
  active dry yeast
½ tsp salt
½ tsp pepper

Cook potatoes in boiling water for 15 minutes or until tender. Drain, reserving 1¼ cups of potato water. Pour into a large bowl adding rosemary, and allowing to cool until tepid. Add yeast and leave 5 to 10 minutes to dissolve. Add flour, salt, and pepper to yeast mixture and stir to make a firm dough. Knead on lightly floured board for 15 to 20 minutes or until dough is smooth. Mash potatoes and work into dough. Place dough in a large, clean bowl, cover with kitchen towel and allow to rise 1 hour or until doubled in size. Punch down and shape into round loaf and place on greased baking sheet. Allow to rise again until doubled in size, about 30 minutes. Preheat oven to 350° about 15 minutes before end of rising time. Bake 45 to 50 minutes or until top of loaf is brown and bottom sounds hollow when tapped.

Irish Soda Bread

4 c flour	1 tsp salt
1 c dark raisins	2 c buttermilk
1 c golden raisins	1 egg
¼ c sugar	Honey Butter
1 tsp baking soda	(recipe follows)

Preheat oven to 350° and grease 9-inch round cake pan. Stir together flour, dark raisins, golden raisins, sugar, baking soda, and salt in a large bowl until well mixed. Make a well in the center. In another bowl, combine buttermilk and egg. Beat until well blended and pour into well of flour mixture. Using your hands, mix thoroughly. Mound dough into prepared pan and smooth top with hands. To ensure even baking, score a cross on top of loaf. Bake until a golden crust forms and loaf sounds hollow when tapped, about 1 hour. Cool and serve warm or at room temperature with Honey Butter.

HONEY BUTTER

2 sticks (8 ozs) butter, softened	½ to ⅔ c honey, to taste

Blend butter and honey in a food processor or blender. Chill until barely firm and shape into 2 to 4 cylinders. Seal in plastic wrap. May be refrigerated for up to 10 days.

Cinnamon, Raisin, and Walnut Batter Bread

1 envelope (¼ oz) active dry yeast	1 tsp cinnamon
1½ c warm water (105°–115°)	1 tsp salt
2 tbsp honey	2 tbsp butter, softened
2 c whole wheat flour	1 c raisins
1 c all-purpose flour	½ c chopped toasted walnuts

Place water in large bowl and dissolve yeast. Whisk, add honey. Add whole wheat flour, all-purpose flour, cinnamon, and salt, and mix until well blended. Stir in butter, raisins, and walnuts and mix well. Place dough in bowl to rise and cover with a kitchen towel. Leave until doubled in size, about 40 to 50 minutes. With a spoon, stir dough down and transfer to well-greased 9x5x3-inch loaf pan. Cover and allow to rise in a warm place for about 20 to 30 minutes, or until dough has reached top of pan. Preheat oven to 400° about 15 minutes before end of rising time. Bake for 30 to 35 minutes, or until loaf bottom sounds hollow when tapped and top of bread is golden. Remove from pan immediately and cool on rack.

Gingerbread Muffins

½ c buttermilk
1 tsp baking soda
¾ c solid vegetable
  shortening
½ c granulated sugar
½ c packed dark
  brown sugar

2 eggs
½ c dark corn syrup
2 c flour
2 tsp ground ginger
1½ tsp cinnamon
½ tsp ground allspice
½ tsp ground cloves

Pour buttermilk in a small bowl; add baking soda, and dissolve, stirring to blend. In a separate bowl at medium speed, beat shortening, granulated sugar, and brown sugar for about 5 minutes, or until light and fluffy. Add eggs one at a time while continuing to blend with electric mixer. Blend in corn syrup. Sift together flour, ginger, cinnamon, allspice, and cloves in a medium bowl. Add to butter mixture, alternating with buttermilk mixture, being sure to beat well after each addition. Cover and refrigerate for 24 hours. Preheat oven to 350°. Grease muffin tins and spoon in batter, filling cups about ¾ full. Bake 20 to 25 minutes, or until only moist crumbs cling to knife inserted into muffins. Yields 24 muffins.

Holiday Streusel Coffee Cake

2 c all-purpose flour
1 c sugar
3 tsp baking powder
1 tsp salt
⅔ c cut-up candied fruit

⅓ c margarine or
   butter, softened
1 c milk
1 egg

Heat oven to 350°. Prepare Streusel and set aside. Combine all of dry ingredients above in mixing bowl. Cut in softened margarine; then add milk and egg and blend on low speed for 30 seconds. Beat at medium speed for 2 minutes, scraping bowl occasionally. Stir in candied fruit and spread batter in greased 13x9x2-inch baking pan. Sprinkle with Streusel. Bake for 35 to 40 minutes or when wooden toothpick inserted in center comes out clean. Yields 12 servings.

STREUSEL

½ c chopped nuts
⅓ c packed brown
   sugar
¼ c all-purpose flour

½ tsp ground cinnamon
3 tbsp firm
   margarine or
   butter

Mix all ingredients above until crumbly.

Mincemeat Coffee Ring

2 c all-purpose flour
2 tbsp sugar
3 tsp baking powder
1 tsp salt
⅔ c milk

⅓ c vegetable oil
1 c prepared
   mincemeat
Lemon Glaze

Heat oven to 425°. Combine flour, sugar, baking powder, and salt. Stir in milk and oil until dough is scraped away from sides of bowl and mounds up into a ball. Knead lightly 10 times. On a lightly floured surface, shape into a 9x13-inch rectangle. Spread mincemeat over top and roll up tightly, beginning at 13-inch side. To seal, pinch edge of dough into roll. Shape into ring on lightly greased cookie sheet with sealed edge down and pinch ends together. Make cuts ⅔ of the way through ring with oiled scissors at 1-inch intervals. Turn each section on its side and bake for 20 to 25 minutes or until golden brown. Spread with Lemon Glaze while warm. Makes 8 to 10 servings.

LEMON GLAZE
Add 1 to 2 teaspoons lemon juice to ½ cup powdered sugar and beat until smooth.

Pumpkin Muffins

1 c packed brown sugar
¾ c vegetable oil
3 eggs
1½ c canned
   pumpkin puree
3½ c flour
2 tsp baking powder
1 tsp baking soda
1 tsp cinnamon

1 tsp grated nutmeg
½ tsp ground cloves
¼ tsp salt
1 c unsweetened
   apple juice
½ c chopped
   toasted walnuts
½ c raisins

Preheat oven to 375°. Line muffin tin with 18 paper baking cups. Beat brown sugar and oil in a large bowl with electric mixer until light and fluffy. Add eggs, one at a time, beating well after each addition. Add pumpkin puree and blend well. In another bowl, gently mix flour, baking powder, baking soda, cinnamon, nutmeg, cloves, and salt. Add apple juice and dry mixture alternately to pumpkin mixture, beginning and ending with dry ingredients. Mix in walnuts and raisins. Pour batter into muffin cups and bake 20 to 25 minutes or until tops are golden and bounce back when touched.

Yogurt and Blueberry Scones

3 c flour
2 tsp baking powder
1 tsp baking soda
½ tsp salt
2 tbsp brown sugar
6 tbsp cold butter

1¼ c plain yogurt
2 eggs
½ c blueberries,
   fresh or frozen
¼ tsp cinnamon

Preheat oven to 400°. Grease a cookie sheet and set aside. Combine flour, baking powder, baking soda, salt, and brown sugar in a medium bowl. Stir gently until well mixed. Using largest holes of a box grater, grate cold butter into flour mixture and stir in as you grate to avoid butter sticking together. Create a well in center and add 1 egg and yogurt. Stir in blueberries dusted with cinnamon until just combined. Scoop dough onto cookie sheet using a ¼-cup measure. Beat remaining egg and brush on top of each scone. Bake 12 to 15 minutes, or until golden brown, and serve immediately.

• • •

*I will honor Christmas in my heart,
and try to keep it all the year.*

CHARLES DICKENS

101
Christmas Recipe Ideas

Main Dishes

Chicken Sausage Stuffing

4 tbsp vegetable oil
1 lb chicken or
   turkey sausage,
   removed from casing
1 large onion, chopped
2 celery ribs, chopped
3 c cubed stale
   pumpernickel bread

2 large eggs
1 turkey (10–12 lbs)
   thawed if frozen
1 tsp sage
1 tsp paprika
½ tsp salt
¼ tsp pepper
2 c chicken broth

Heat 2 tablespoons oil in a large skillet over medium heat. Add sausage and cook 5 to 7 minutes or until lightly browned. Turn into large bowl and set aside. Heat remaining 2 tablespoons oil in same frying pan and add onion and celery, cooking 3 to 5 minutes or until tender. Add to bowl with sausage and cool. Mix eggs and bread well. Preheat oven to 350°. Remove neck and giblets from turkey and rinse turkey inside and out. Pat dry and season turkey with sage, paprika, salt, and pepper. Stuff loosely with filling. Place turkey in large roasting pan with breast side up. Pour chicken broth around turkey and roast for 3½ to 4 hours, or until bird is tender and juices run clear when thigh is pricked with a fork. Baste every 30 minutes.

Roast Beef with Yorkshire Pudding

Place 4- to 6-pound boneless rib roast on rack in shallow roasting pan with fat side up. Sprinkle with salt and pepper and insert meat thermometer in thickest part of beef, avoiding fat. Roast in oven at 325° uncovered for about 1¾ hours to desired degree of doneness: 130–135° for rare, and 150–155° for medium. Shortly before beef is done, prepare Yorkshire Pudding Batter (recipe follows). Remove beef from oven and transfer to platter; cover with aluminum foil. Heat a 9x9x2-inch baking pan in oven at 425°. Reserve ¼ cup meat drippings, adding vegetable oil if necessary, and pour into heated pan. Add pudding batter and bake 25 minutes or until puffed and golden brown. Cut into squares and serve with sliced roast beef.

Yorkshire Pudding Batter

1 c all-purpose flour	2 eggs
1 c milk	½ tsp salt

Beat all ingredients until smooth.

Ginger Beef

3 tbsp oil   ⅓ c thinly sliced ginger
1 lb beef steak   2 tbsp oyster sauce

Measure oil. Slice steak into pieces 2 inches long by 1 inch wide by ¼ inch thick. Measure ginger and oyster sauce. Set by the stove in order listed. Set wok over high heat for 30 seconds; swirl in oil; heat to almost smoking; add beef and stir-fry 1 minute. Add ginger, and stir-fry 4 minutes. Add oyster sauce and stir-fry 2 minutes more. Serve at once.

Herbed Salmon Steaks

2 tbsp margarine   ¼ tsp pepper
   or butter   ½ tsp dried marjoram
2 tbsp lemon juice   or thyme leaves
4 salmon steaks,   paprika
   ¾-inch thick   lemon wedges
1 tsp onion salt   parsley

Place margarine and lemon juice in a 12x7½x2-inch baking dish and heat at 400°. Coat both sides of fish with lemon butter and place in baking dish. Sprinkle with seasonings and bake uncovered about 25 minutes, or until fish flakes easily with fork. Sprinkle with paprika and serve with lemon wedges and parsley. Serves 4.

Savory Pork Roast

4-lb pork boneless top loin roast	1 tsp dried sage leaves
1 clove garlic, cut into halves	1 tsp dried marjoram leaves
	1 tsp salt

Using cut sides of garlic, rub pork roast. After mixing remaining ingredients, sprinkle on roast and place fat side up in shallow roasting pan. Insert meat thermometer in thickest part of pork and roast uncovered at 325° for 2 to 2½ hours, or until meat thermometer registers 170°. Garnish with frosted grapes (dipped in water and rolled in sugar) if desired.

• • •

It came upon the midnight clear,
that glorious song of old,
From angels bending near the earth,
to touch their harps of gold;
"Peace on the earth, good will to men,
from heaven's all gracious King."
The world in solemn stillness lay,
to hear the angels sing.

EDMUND H. SEARS,
"It Came Upon the Midnight Clear"

Roast Goose with Browned Potatoes

1 goose (9 to 11 lbs)
4 to 6 large potatoes,
    pared and cut
    into halves

salt and pepper
paprika

Remove excess fat from goose. Lightly rub salt into cavity of goose. With skewer, fasten neck skin to back. Fold wings across back with tips touching and tie drumsticks to tail. Pierce skin liberally with fork. Place goose in shallow roasting pan breast side up and roast uncovered at 350° for 3 to 3½ hours, removing excess fat from pan occasionally. One hour and 15 minutes before goose is done, place potatoes around goose in roasting pan. Brush potatoes with goose drippings and sprinkle with salt, pepper, and paprika. Place a tent of aluminum foil loosely over goose to prevent excessive browning if necessary. After baking, cover and let stand 15 minutes for easier carving.

HERBED CORNISH HENS

3 frozen Rock Cornish
hens (about 1 lb
each), thawed
¼ c margarine
or butter,
melted

½ tsp dried marjoram
leaves
½ tsp dried thyme
leaves
¼ tsp paprika
salt and pepper

Rub salt and pepper into cavities of hens. Combine margarine, marjoram, thyme, and paprika; brush portion of mixture on hens that have been placed in shallow baking pan, breast side up. Roast uncovered at 350°, brushing with remaining margarine mixture 5 or 6 times until done (about 1 hour). Cut each hen into halves with scissors, cutting along backbone from tail to neck and down center of breast. Garnish with watercress.

• • •

Fear not: for, behold,
I bring you good tidings of great joy,
which shall be to all people.
For unto you is born this day
in the city of David a Saviour,
which is Christ the Lord.

LUKE 2:10–11

Honey Roast Ham

4½-pound cured ham,
   leg or shoulder roast
1 onion
cloves
2 bay leaves
a few black peppercorns

twist of orange peel
small piece of fresh
   ginger
½ cinnamon stick
a few stalks of parsley

Glaze

cloves
6 tbsp clear honey

2 tbsp whole grain
   mustard

Calculate cooking time for ham, figuring 20 minutes per pound, adding an extra 20 minutes. In order to draw off salt used in curing process, place ham in a large pan and cover with cold water. Bring to a boil and remove from heat. Pour off water and replace with cold water, adding onion, cloves, and other flavoring ingredients. Bring to a boil slowly, cover and simmer for calculated time, subtracting 15 minutes. Remove ham from pan and cool slightly. Heat oven to 350°. Score fat of ham in diamond pattern with sharp knife and press cloves into fat at intervals. Combine honey and mustard and spread over skin. Wrap ham in foil, leaving glazed area uncovered. Bake in roasting pan for 15 minutes. Serve hot or cold. Serves 8 to 10.

Lasagna

1 pound Italian sausage
1 clove garlic, minced
1 tbsp whole basil
1½ tsp salt
1 can (1 lb) tomatoes
2 cans (6 ozs) tomato paste
10 ozs lasagna noodles
2 eggs
1 lb mozzarella cheese,
  sliced very thin

3 c fresh ricotta
  or cream-style
  cottage cheese
½ c grated
  Parmesan or
  Romano cheese
2 tbsp parsley flakes
1 tsp salt
½ tsp pepper

Brown sausage slowly and spoon off excess fat. Add next 5 ingredients plus 1 cup of water and simmer, covered, for 15 minutes; stir frequently. Cook noodles in boiling salted water till tender. Beat eggs and add remaining ingredients except mozzarella. Layer half the lasagna noodles in 9x13x2-inch baking dish; spread with half of ricotta filling; then half of mozzarella cheese and half of meat sauce. Repeat. Bake at 375° for 30 minutes. Serves 8 to 10.

101
Christmas Recipe Ideas

Side Dishes

Scalloped Oysters

2 c oyster crackers
1 pt oysters
½ c heavy cream
¼ tsp salt

⅛ tsp freshly
  ground pepper
1 tbsp chopped parsley
2 tbsp butter

Preheat oven to 425°. Grease a 9x13-inch baking dish, placing half of crackers on bottom layer. Top with oysters. Drizzle ¼ cup cream over oysters and season with half of salt and pepper. Sprinkle with chopped parsley and spread remaining crackers, cream, salt, and pepper over top. Dot with butter and bake 20 to 25 minutes or until bubbly and lightly browned.

Duchess Potatoes

instant mashed potatoes
paprika

1 egg

Prepare instant mashed potatoes to serve four according to package directions, but decrease milk to 2 tablespoons. In a small bowl, beat 1 egg slightly; add hot potatoes and beat at medium speed until fluffy. Drop by teaspoonfuls onto greased cookie sheet and sprinkle with paprika. Bake at 400° for about 15 minutes or until golden brown.

Holiday Salad

2 c boiling water
1 package (6 ozs)
    lime-flavored gelatin
1 can (20 ozs) crushed
    pineapple, drained
    (reserve syrup)
1 package (8 ozs)
    cream cheese, softened

¾ c whipping
    cream
½ c finely
    chopped celery
2 tbsp mayonnaise
    or salad dressing
salad greens

Place gelatin in a 1½-quart bowl and pour boiling water over top. Stir until dissolved. Add enough water to reserved pineapple syrup to measure 1 cup and stir into gelatin. Pour ½ cup gelatin into a 7-cup mold or baking pan, 9x9x2 inches. Chill until firm. Blend remaining gelatin into cream cheese until smooth. Refrigerate for 1 to 1½ hours or until slightly thickened. Beat until smooth. In another chilled bowl, beat whipping cream until stiff. Fold mayonnaise, celery, whipped cream, and pineapple into gelatin mixture and pour out over gelatin in mold. Chill 2 hours or until firm. Remove salad from mold onto salad greens.

Ham and Broccoli Scallop

1 package (5½ ozs) au gratin potato mix
1½ to 2 c cubed fully cooked smoked ham
1 package (10 ozs) frozen chopped broccoli,
    partially thawed and broken apart

Prepare potatoes according to package directions, but omit margarine and use casserole. Stir in ham and broccoli. Cook uncovered 45 to 50 minutes.

Oyster Stew

3 tbsp unsalted butter   ¼ tsp white pepper
2 pts fresh oysters   pinch cayenne
½ tsp salt   2 c milk
¼ tsp ground mace   2 c light cream

Melt butter in a large heavy saucepan over medium-low heat. Add oysters and seasonings. Cook about 5 minutes, or until oysters plump up and edges just begin to curl. In another saucepan, cook milk and cream over medium heat being careful not to boil or scorch. Add hot milk mixture to cooked oysters, mixing well, and serve at once in heated bowls. Serves 6 to 8.

White and Wild Rice Medley

½ c slivered almonds
¼ c uncooked wild rice
1 jar (2½ ozs) sliced
   mushrooms, drained
2 tbsp chopped green
   onions
¼ c margarine or butter

1 tbsp instant
   chicken bouillon
2½ c boiling
   water
¾ c uncooked
   regular rice

Melt margarine in skillet and add almonds, wild rice, mushrooms, and green onion. Cook and stir for 10 to 15 minutes until almonds are golden brown. Pour into ungreased 1½-quart casserole. Stir in instant bouillon and water. Cover and cook at 350° for 30 minutes. Mix in regular rice. Cover and cook about 30 minutes longer until liquid is absorbed. Serves 6.

• • •

So glad hearts on this happy Christmas night
Bring your gifts of love, make His altar bright;
Sing glad songs that shall sweetly sound as when
Angels sang of peace and good will to men.

MARY B. SLADE,
"Beautiful Christmas"

Fresh Cranberry Salad

2 c water
¾ c sugar
3 c (12 ozs)
    cranberries
1 package (6 ozs)
    orange-flavored gelatin

1 can (8¼ ozs)
    crushed pineapple
½ c chopped
    celery or walnuts
salad greens

Place water and sugar in a 2-quart saucepan and bring to a boil; boil 1 minute. Add cranberries and return to a boil for 5 minutes. Add gelatin and stir until dissolved. Stir in celery and pineapple (including liquid). Pour into a 6-cup mold and chill at least 6 hours until firm. Unmold on salad greens. May be garnished with pineapple chunks and sour cream.

Apple Sauce

2 large cooking apples,
    peeled, cored, and
    chopped
2 tbsp apple juice
1 tbsp butter

1 tbsp light brown
    sugar
1 star anise seedpod
salt and freshly
    ground black pepper

Place all ingredients except salt and pepper in pan and cook over medium heat, uncovered for 15 minutes, stirring occasionally until fruit is soft. Remove the star anise and puree fruit in a food processor. Season with salt and pepper.

Roast Goose Gravy

giblets from goose, washed
1 onion, skinned and
   quartered
4 cloves
½ lemon, roughly cut
slice of orange peel
1 stalk celery, sliced

1 carrot, sliced
4⅔ c water
1 tbsp all-purpose
   flour
salt and freshly
   ground black
   pepper

Place first 7 ingredients in a pan and cover with water. Bring to a boil and skim off foam that rises to surface. Cover and simmer for 1 hour. With juices reserved from roasted goose, stir in flour over low heat. Add stock from first mixture and stir until gravy is smooth and thick.

Roast Beef Gravy

1 tbsp all-purpose flour

1½ c meat or
   vegetable stock

Pour off fat from roasting pan and add flour to remaining drippings. Stir over medium heat gradually pouring in stock. Bring to a boil and season with salt and pepper.

Roast and Pecan Stuffing for Goose

1 large onion, chopped
6 stalks celery,
   finely chopped
3 tbsp water
1½ c fresh white
   bread crumbs
⅔ c seedless raisins
1 c pecans, chopped

grated rind and juice
   of 1 orange
2 eggs, beaten
grated nutmeg
salt
freshly ground
   black pepper

Simmer onion and celery in small pan with water for about 5 minutes until tender. Place vegetables in a bowl and stir in bread crumbs, raisins, nuts, orange rind, juice, and eggs. Season to taste with nutmeg, salt, and pepper. Allow to cool, then pack in goose.

• • •

Hark! The herald angels sing,
"Glory to the newborn King;
Peace on earth, and mercy mild,
God and sinners reconciled!"
Joyful, all ye nations rise,
Join the triumph of the skies;
With th'angelic host proclaim,
"Christ is born in Bethlehem!"

CHARLES WESLEY,
"Hark! The Herald Angels Sing"

101
Christmas Recipe Ideas

Cookies

Chocolate-Almond Teacakes

¾ c margarine or butter, softened
⅓ c powdered sugar
1 c all-purpose flour
powdered sugar

½ c instant cocoa mix
½ c toasted diced almonds

Combine margarine and ⅓ cup powdered sugar. Stir in flour, cocoa mix, and almonds. (Refrigerate until firm if dough is too soft to shape.) Heat oven to 325°. Shape dough into 1-inch balls and place on an ungreased cookie sheet. Bake about 20 minutes, or until set. Dip tops into powdered sugar while still warm. Let cool and dip again. Yields 4 dozen cookies.

• • •

What is Christmas?
It is tenderness for the past,
courage for the present,
hope for the future.
It is a fervent wish that
every cup may overflow with
blessings rich and eternal,
and that every path may lead to peace.

AGNES M. PHARO

French Christmas Cookies

½ c butter or other
shortening (softened)
¾ c sugar
½ c honey

2 egg yolks
¼ c milk
1 tsp vanilla
3 c sifted
cake flour

Cream butter and sugar together until light. Add honey and egg yolks, beating well after each addition. Add milk and vanilla. Add flour in small amounts until well blended. Chill dough for 2 hours. Roll ⅛ inch thick on lightly floured board. Cut into desired shapes and bake on ungreased cookie sheets for 10 minutes at 375°. Cool and frost. Yields 3 dozen cookies.

• • •

*From home to home,
and heart to heart,
from one place to another. . .
The warmth and joy of Christmas,
brings us closer to each other. . . .*

EMILY MATTHEWS

Turtle Cookies

½ c packed brown sugar
½ c margarine or butter,
  softened
2 tbsp water
1 tsp vanilla
1½ c all-purpose flour

⅛ tsp salt
pecan halves
8 caramels, each
  cut into fourths
Chocolate Glaze

Combine brown sugar, margarine, water, and vanilla. Stir in flour and salt until dough holds together. (Add 1 to 2 teaspoons of water if dough is dry.) Heat oven to 350°. Place 3 to 5 pecan halves in a group for each cookie on an ungreased cookie sheet. Shape dough by teaspoonfuls around caramel pieces; press firmly onto the center of each group of nuts. Bake until set, but do not brown, for 12 to 15 minutes. Cool; then dip tops of cookies into Chocolate Glaze. Yields 2½ dozen cookies.

CHOCOLATE GLAZE

In a separate bowl, beat 1 cup of confectioners' sugar, 1 tablespoon water, 1 ounce melted unsweetened chocolate (cool), and 1 teaspoon vanilla until smooth. Stir in water, 1 teaspoon at a time, until frosting reaches desired consistency.

Magic Window Cookies

1 c sugar
¾ c shortening
(part margarine or
butter, softened)
2 eggs
1 tsp vanilla or ½ tsp
lemon extract

2½ c all-purpose flour
1 tsp baking powder
1 tsp salt
about 5 rolls
(about .79 oz each)
ring-shaped
hard candy

Combine sugar, shortening, eggs, and vanilla. Add flour, baking powder, and salt. Cover and refrigerate at least 1 hour. On a lightly floured cloth-covered board, roll dough ⅛ inch thick. Cut into desired shapes with cookie cutters. Place cookies on a cookie sheet that has been covered with aluminum foil. Using smaller cutters, cut out centers of cookies and place whole or partially crushed candy in remaining center. (Since candy melts easily, there is no need to crush it finely.) If cookies will be hung from Christmas tree to enjoy "stained-glass" effect, make a hole ¼ inch from top with the end of a plastic straw. Heat oven to 375°. Bake 7 to 9 minutes, or until cookies are very light brown and candy is melted. If candy has not filled out cutout center, spread immediately with a metal spatula. Cool completely on cookie sheet. Yields 6 dozen 3-inch cookies.

Thumbprints

1 stick unsalted butter, softened	1 egg
½ c peanut butter	2 tbsp milk
1¼ c sugar	2 c flour
	⅔ c raspberry jam

Using an electric mixer, beat together butter and peanut butter. Add sugar and beat until fluffy; then beat in egg and milk. Add flour, stirring with a spoon until a thick dough is formed. Place in a small, covered bowl and refrigerate at least 2 hours or until well chilled. Preheat oven to 350°. Roll dough into 1-inch balls and place 2 inches apart on a buttered cookie sheet. Gently flatten balls with the palm of your hand and make a small indentation in each with thumbtip. Fill each indentation with ½ teaspoon of jam. Bake for 13 to 15 minutes, or until edges are lightly browned.

• • •

Blessed is the season which engages the whole world in a conspiracy of love.

HAMILTON WRIGHT MABIE

Snowtime Ginger Cookies

1¼ c sugar
1 c butter or margarine, softened
1 egg
3 tbsp dark corn syrup
1 tsp vanilla

3 c flour
1½ tsp baking soda
2 tsp cinnamon
1 tsp ginger
¼ tsp salt
¼ tsp cloves

Mix sugar and butter at medium speed for 1 to 2 minutes until well mixed. Beat in egg, corn syrup, and vanilla for another 1 to 2 minutes. Reduce speed and add flour, baking soda, cinnamon, ginger, salt, and cloves. Divide dough into three parts and shape each part into a ball, then flatten balls to ½ inch. Wrap dough in plastic wrap and refrigerate for 1 to 2 hours. Roll out dough to ⅛ inch, one-third at a time. Cut with 2- to 3-inch cookie cutters and place on an ungreased cookie sheet, one inch apart. Bake for 5 to 7 minutes at 375°. Makes about 7 dozen cookies.

Candy Cane Twists

1½ c powdered sugar
1¼ c butter or
     margarine, softened
1 egg
1 tsp peppermint extract
1 tsp vanilla

2¾ c flour
¼ tsp salt
⅓ c finely crushed
     candy canes, or
     peppermint candy
¼ tsp red food
     coloring

Beat powdered sugar, butter, egg, peppermint extract, and vanilla together at medium speed until creamy. Reduce speed and add flour and salt. Divide dough in half. Stir candy into one half of the dough and beat food coloring into the other half. For each cookie, roll 1 teaspoon of each dough into a 4-inch long rope. Place ropes beside each other and twist them together. Place on an ungreased cookie sheet and curve one end of cookie to make the shape of a candy cane. Bake at 350° for 10 to 12 minutes. Makes about 4½ dozen cookies.

• • •

Peace on earth will come to stay,
When we live Christmas every day.

HELEN STEINER RICE

Double Mint Chocolate Cookies

1 c sugar
½ c cocoa
1 egg
½ c butter or margarine,
   softened
½ tsp vanilla

2 c flour
1 tsp baking soda
1 tsp baking powder
¼ tsp salt
½ c buttermilk
½ c water

Frosting

2 c powdered sugar
1 to 2 tbsp milk
½ tsp salt
½ c butter or
   margarine, softened

1 tsp vanilla
¼ tsp mint extract
¼ c crushed
   peppermint candy

Mix sugar, cocoa, egg, butter, and vanilla at medium speed until well mixed. At reduced speed, add flour, baking soda, baking powder, and salt a little at a time. Alternately add buttermilk and water. Drop dough by rounded teaspoons onto a greased cookie sheet, 2 inches apart. Bake at 400° for 7 to 9 minutes. Cool completely. Combine all frosting ingredients except candy. Beat until creamy. Spread about 1 tablespoon of frosting on top of each cookie and sprinkle with crushed candy. Makes about 4 dozen cookies.

Chocolate Holiday Cookies

⅔ c powdered sugar
½ c butter or margarine,
   softened
½ tsp vanilla

1 c flour
2 tbsp cocoa
⅛ tsp salt

Icing

1¼ c powdered sugar
1 tbsp meringue powder

2 tbsp warm water
¼ tsp cream of tartar

Beat together powdered sugar, butter, and vanilla at medium speed. Reduce speed and add flour, cocoa, and salt. Divide dough in half. One half at a time, place dough between sheets of lightly floured waxed paper and roll out to ⅛-inch thickness, refrigerating remaining half. Remove paper and cut with 2- to 2½-inch cookie cutters. Place on an ungreased cookie sheet. Bake at 325° for 14 to 18 minutes.

Combine icing ingredients and beat at low speed until moistened. Increase speed and beat until stiff and glossy. Add more warm water if icing becomes too stiff. Cover with damp paper towel until ready to use. Cool cookies completely before decorating with icing as desired. Makes about 2 dozen cookies.

Nutmeg Butterfingers

1 c butter or margarine,
    softened
¾ c sugar
1 egg

2 tsp vanilla
3 c flour
¼ tsp nutmeg

FROSTING

2 c powdered sugar
⅓ c butter or margarine,
    softened
1 tbsp nutmeg

1 tsp vanilla
2 tsp rum-flavored
    extract, if desired

Mix butter and sugar at medium speed until creamy. Add egg and vanilla. Reduce speed and add flour and nutmeg. Form dough into 3½-inch fingers and place on a greased cookie sheet. Bake at 350° for 13 to 15 minutes. Beat together all frosting ingredients. Spread frosting on cooled cookies. Sprinkle lightly with nutmeg. Makes about 6 dozen cookies.

Double Delights

1 c sugar	1 tsp baking powder
¾ c butter or	¼ tsp salt
margarine, softened	2 (1-oz) squares
1 egg	unsweetened baking
2 tsp vanilla	chocolate, melted
2¼ c flour	

Beat sugar and butter together at medium speed until creamy. Add egg and vanilla. Reduce speed and add flour, baking powder, and salt. Divide dough into two parts. Wrap half the dough in waxed paper. Add melted chocolate to remaining half and beat at low speed until just mixed. Wrap chocolate dough in waxed paper. Refrigerate both halves for at least an hour. Shape rounded teaspoons of dough into desired shapes, using both doughs. Place on an ungreased cookie sheet, 1 inch apart. Bake at 375° for 7 to 8 minutes. Decorate as desired after cooling. Makes about 3 dozen cookies.

Cinnamon Blossoms

1 c butter or margarine,
    softened
¾ c sugar
1 egg yolk
1 tsp vanilla

2 c flour
1½ tsp cinnamon
¼ tsp salt
60 mini chocolate
    kisses

Combine butter, sugar, egg yolk, and vanilla, beating on medium speed until creamy. Reduce speed and add flour, cinnamon, and salt. Fill cookie press with dough. Press dough onto an ungreased cookie sheet, 1 inch apart. Bake at 375° for 8 to 11 minutes. As soon as cookies are removed from the oven, place 1 chocolate in the center of each. Makes 5 dozen cookies.

• • •

fall on your knees,
    O hear the angel voices!
O night divine,
    O night when Christ was born!
O night, O holy night,
    O night divine!

PLACIDE CLAPPEAU,
"O Holy Night"

Orange Pistachio Butter Balls

1 c butter or
   margarine, softened
½ c powdered sugar
2 c flour
2 tsp grated orange peel

1 c finely
   chopped, salted
   pistachio nuts
2 tsp vanilla
powdered sugar

Mix butter and powdered sugar at medium speed until creamy. Reduce speed and add flour, orange peel, nuts, and vanilla. Form dough into 1-inch balls. Place balls on an ungreased cookie sheet, 1 inch apart. Bake at 350° for 9 to 11 minutes. Roll cookies in powdered sugar while still warm and again after being cooled. Makes about 5 dozen cookies.

• • •

*Are you willing to believe that love is
the strongest thing in the world—
stronger than hate, stronger than evil,
stronger than death—
and that the blessed life which
began in Bethlehem nineteen hundred years ago
is the image and brightness of the Eternal Love?
Then you can keep Christmas.*

HENRY VAN DYKE

Angel Cookies

1 c sugar
1 c butter or margarine,
   softened
1 egg
1 tsp vanilla
½ tsp almond extract

2 c flour
½ tsp baking soda
½ tsp cream of tartar
¼ tsp salt
water
sugar

Beat together sugar and butter at medium speed until creamy. Add egg, vanilla, and almond extract, beating well. Reduce speed and add flour, baking soda, cream of tartar, and salt. Shape dough into 1-inch balls. Dip the top of each ball into water, then into sugar. Place the balls on an ungreased cookie sheet, 2 inches apart. Bake at 375° for 7 to 9 minutes. Makes about 3 dozen cookies.

Spritz Surprise Cookies

1 (8-oz) package
  individually wrapped,
  assorted miniature
  chocolate bars
  (¼ oz each)
⅔ c sugar

1 c butter or
  margarine, softened
1 tbsp vanilla
1 egg
2¼ c flour

Mix sugar, butter, vanilla, and egg at medium speed until creamy. Reduce speed and add flour. Fill cookie press with dough and attach ribbon template. Press half the dough onto ungreased cookie sheets in 14½-inch long ribbons. Break chocolate bars into ¾- to 1-inch pieces and place on strips of dough, ½ inch apart. Press remaining dough in ribbons over candy. Mark dough between chocolate pieces with a table knife. Bake at 375° for 10 to 15 minutes. While cookies are still warm, cut or break them apart at marks. Makes about 4½ dozen cookies.

• • •

*He who has not Christmas in his heart
will never find it under a tree.*

Roy L. Smith

Norwegian Cookies

1⅓ c sugar
1 c butter or margarine,
  softened
2 eggs
1 tsp vanilla

3 c flour
1 tsp baking powder
1 (12-oz) package
  semisweet
  chocolate chips
  (2 c)

TOPPING

3 tbsp sugar   ¾ tsp cinnamon

Mix sugar and butter together at medium speed until creamy. Beat in eggs and vanilla. Reduce speed and add flour and baking powder. Stir in chocolate chips by hand. Divide dough in half on a lightly floured surface. Divide each half into thirds and shape each of the parts into a 10-inch roll. Place 2 rolls per ungreased cookie sheet, at least 2 inches apart. Flatten each roll with a moistened fork to about ½ inch thick. Combine sugar and cinnamon and sprinkle about ½ tsp of mixture on each roll. Bake at 350° for 13 to 15 minutes. Slice diagonally into 1-inch strips while still warm. Makes about 6 dozen cookies.

101
Christmas Recipe Ideas

Desserts

Epiphany Jam Tart

4 to 4½ c flour
½ tsp salt
⅔ c sugar, sieved
½ tsp cinnamon
1½ c (¾ lb)
  unsalted butter, slightly softened
different-colored thick jams: strawberry, raspberry,
  gooseberry, orange marmalade, pineapple,
  quince, prune, etc.
1 egg yolk beaten with 1 tbsp milk

2 eggs
4 hard-boiled egg yolks
2 to 4 tbsp milk
grated rind of 1 lemon

Sift together dry ingredients into a wide bowl and cut butter into mixture, using a pastry blender, until mixture resembles fine meal. Stir together eggs, yolks, milk, and lemon rind, and pour into a well in center of flour mixture. Using a fork, work ingredients together until dough sticks together in a ball. Knead dough until smooth and wrap in waxed paper; chill for 30 minutes. Divide dough into two equal parts. Roll out first between waxed paper to ¼-inch thickness and place in bottom of pie plate. Roll out other half in circle of the same size. From this, cut a 1-inch ring that will fit around edge of pie plate. Cut remaining dough into strips to form star pattern across pie plate and secure with already cut ring of pastry around pie plate. Spoon as many different-colored jams as possible into spaces between lattice strips; brush strips with egg yolk glaze and bake in oven preheated to 350° for 30 to 45 minutes. Makes a 9-inch tart.

Bûche de Noël

Yule Log Cake

1 c flour	4 eggs
1¼ tsp baking powder	⅔ c sugar
¼ tsp salt	1 tbsp hot water
1 tbsp cocoa	

Filling

½ c butter or margarine	2 tbsp cocoa
2¼ c powdered sugar	2 to 3 tbsp milk

Sift together flour, baking powder, salt, and cocoa. In a bowl over a pan of hot water, whisk together eggs and sugar until pale and thick. Remove from heat and fold in half the flour mixture. Fold in remaining flour mixture, along with hot water. Pour batter into a lined jelly roll pan. Bake at 425° for about 10 minutes. Turn cake onto a sheet of waxed paper and trim edges of cake. Before it cools, roll up cake with the paper inside. Set aside to cool. For filling, mix butter and powdered sugar. Beat in cocoa and milk until mixture is fluffy. Unroll cake and remove paper. Spread ¼ of filling on cake and roll it up. Spread the rest of the filling on the outside of the log. Use a fork to make swirls and ridges like tree bark. Decorate with powdered sugar, if desired.

Pán de Pascua

Christmas Cake

1 c butter or margarine
1½ tbsp warm water
2 c powdered sugar
6 eggs, separated
1 c seedless raisins
1⅓ c mixed
   crystallized fruits,
   chopped
½ c walnuts,
   broken

4¾ c flour
2 tbsp baking powder
1 tsp cinnamon
¼ tsp nutmeg
2 to 3 whole cloves
2 tbsp rum flavoring
1 tbsp vinegar
1 c milk

Beat butter and warm water until fluffy. Add powdered sugar a little at a time. Beat in egg yolks. Mix in raisins, candied fruits, and walnuts by hand. Stir in flour, baking powder, spices, rum flavoring, and vinegar. Beat egg whites until they form soft peaks, then fold them into the batter. Add enough of the milk so that the batter drops from a spoon, but is not too soft. Pour batter into a greased and lined 8-inch round pan. Bake at 375° for 15 minutes. Lower temperature to 325° and bake for 50 to 55 minutes. Cool for 10 minutes, then remove cake from pan to cool. Sprinkle with powdered sugar before serving.

Puff Pastry

4 c flour	1¾ c butter or
1 tsp salt	margarine
1 tbsp lemon juice	¼ c shortening
12 to 14 tbsp ice water	

Mix flour and salt on a pastry board. Make a well in the center and add lemon juice and 6 tablespoons water. Stir with fingers, mixing in flour. Gradually add more water until flour is all absorbed and dough forms a ball. Knead lightly. Wrap in waxed paper and a damp cloth. Refrigerate 30 minutes. Mix butter and shortening with a spatula. Form into a brick, wrap in waxed paper, and refrigerate. Roll out dough on floured surface, forming a 12-inch circle. Place butter on dough and fold dough around it, sealing edges. Roll into a 16x8-inch rectangle, short side facing you. Fold dough into thirds, sealing edges. Wrap in waxed paper and a damp cloth. Refrigerate 15 minutes. Short side facing you, roll out dough to similar size and repeat procedure. Repeat 8 more times. Wrap pastry and refrigerate overnight. Use as directed. Pastry will keep several days.

Buñuelos Navideños

Christmas Fritters

2 c water	¾ c flour
¼ tsp salt	5 eggs
2 tbsp butter or margarine	oil for frying
4 tbsp cornmeal	

Syrup

1 c sugar	1 tsp lemon juice
1 c water	1 tsp orange flower
4-inch cinnamon stick	water

Boil water, salt, and butter. Add cornmeal and flour and stir over low heat until mixture forms a ball. Put dough in a bowl and beat it with a wooden spoon until it cools. Beat in eggs one at a time. Heat oil to 375° in deep fryer. Drop tablespoons of dough into oil a few at a time. Remove when golden and drain on paper towels. For the syrup, heat sugar and water in saucepan together with the cinnamon stick. After sugar dissolves, boil syrup until it thickens slightly. Turn off heat and remove cinnamon stick. Stir in lemon juice and orange flower water. Arrange fritters on a plate and pour syrup over them.

CRANBERRY APRICOT TARTLETS

TARTLET SHELLS

¼ c sugar

½ c butter or margarine

1 to 3 tbsp orange juice

¼ tsp salt

½ tsp grated orange peels cut into 4 pieces

1⅓ c flour

FILLING

1½ c fresh or frozen cranberries

¾ c dried apricots, chopped

1 c sugar

½ tsp grated orange peel

⅓ c orange juice

¼ c water

sweetened whipped cream, if desired

Combine sugar, butter, flour, and salt, beating at low speed until crumbly. Add orange peel and enough orange juice to form a dough. Divide dough into 30 equal pieces. Press dough onto the bottom and sides of greased and sugared mini-muffin cups. Bake at 375° for 14 to 18 minutes. Loosen edges with a knife and remove shells.

Combine all filling ingredients except whipped cream, cooking over medium-high heat until mixture comes to a full boil. Stir occasionally. Reduce heat to low and cook for 15 to 20 minutes, stirring occasionally, until mixture is thickened. When filling is completely cooled, just before serving, spoon filling into shells. If desired, top with whipped cream. Makes 30 tartlets.

Glistening Fruitcake Jewels

Crumb Mixture

¾ c butter or
   margarine, softened

2 c flour
½ c sugar

Filling

½ c sugar
½ c raisins
¼ c orange or
   lemon juice
1 (8-oz) package
   chopped dates

1 (2½-oz) package
   sliced almonds
1 egg
¼ c candied
   cherries, chopped

Glaze

¾ c powdered sugar
1 tbsp milk

½ tsp vanilla

Beat all ingredients for crumb mixture on low speed until crumbly. Press into the bottom of a greased 9x13-inch pan. Bake at 350° for 15 to 20 minutes. Combine all filling ingredients except cherries. Spread over hot crust and sprinkle with cherries. Bake for 17 to 20 minutes. Mix glaze ingredients and drizzle over cooled bars. Makes about 36 bars.

Strawberry Linzer Bars

1¾ c flour
½ c sugar
1 (2-oz) package hazelnuts
    or blanched almonds,
    ground (½ c)
1 tsp grated lemon peel
½ tsp cinnamon
½ tsp baking powder
¼ tsp salt

½ c butter or
    margarine,
    cut into pieces
1 egg, beaten
1 tsp vanilla
½ c seedless strawberry
    or raspberry jam
powdered sugar
cinnamon

Mix flour, sugar, hazelnuts, lemon peel, cinnamon, baking powder, and salt. Add butter and beat at low speed until crumbly. Beat in egg and vanilla. Divide dough in half. Press half the dough into an ungreased 9-inch square pan. Spread jam on dough to within ½ inch of the edge. Roll out other half of dough between two sheets of floured waxed paper, forming an 11x10-inch rectangle. Remove waxed paper and cut dough into twenty ½-inch strips. Place strips over jam diagonally, forming a lattice crust. Bake at 350° for 23 to 28 minutes. When cool, sprinkle with powdered sugar and cinnamon. Store in the refrigerator. Makes about 36 bars.

ORANGE BUTTER CREAM SQUARES

CRUST

1¼ c chocolate
   wafer cookies, finely
   crushed (about 25)

⅓ c butter or
   margarine,
   softened

FILLING

1½ c powdered sugar
⅓ c butter or margarine
2 tsp grated orange peel

1 tbsp milk
½ tsp vanilla

GLAZE

1 tbsp butter or margarine, melted
1 tbsp cocoa

Stir together all crust ingredients and press into the bottom of an ungreased 9-inch square pan. Cover and refrigerate for about 1 hour. Beat all filling ingredients at medium speed until creamy. Spread over crust.

Mix glaze ingredients and drizzle over filling. Refrigerate for 1 to 2 hours, until firm. Store in refrigerator. Makes about 25 bars.

Vanilla and Chocolate Biscotti

1 c sugar
¼ c butter or
   margarine, softened
2 eggs
2 tsp vanilla
2 c flour
½ c toasted walnuts,
   finely chopped

½ tsp baking powder
½ tsp baking soda
¼ tsp salt
1 (1-oz) square
   unsweetened chocolate
   melted, cooled

DRIZZLE

¼ c semisweet
   chocolate chips

¼ c vanilla milk chips
2 tsp shortening

Mix sugar and butter at medium speed. Add eggs and vanilla. Reduce speed and add flour, walnuts, baking powder, baking soda, and salt. Remove half of dough and add melted chocolate to remaining half. Divide both chocolate and white doughs into half. Roll each part into a 6-inch log. Place 1 chocolate log on top of 1 white log and roll together to form a roll 10x1½ inches. Repeat. Place rolls on an ungreased cookie sheet, 3 inches apart. Bake at 350° for 23 to 25 minutes. Cool about 15 minutes. Cut logs diagonally into ½-inch slices. Arrange on cookie sheet. Bake at 300° for 14 to 18 minutes, turning once, until golden on both sides. Melt chocolate chips and 1 teaspoon shortening over low heat, stirring well. Do the same with vanilla chips and remaining shortening. Drizzle mixtures over cooled biscotti. Makes about 3 dozen biscotti.

Brownie Christmas Trees

1 (19.8- to 21.5-oz) package plain brownie mix
½ c butter or margarine, melted

Frosting

3 c powdered sugar
½ c butter or
   margarine, softened
1 tsp vanilla
3 to 4 tbsp milk
3 to 4 drops green
   food coloring

2 to 3 tbsp miniature
   candy-coated
   chocolate pieces
28 (1- to 1½-inch)
   pretzel rod pieces

Prepare brownie mix according to package directions except substitute melted butter for oil. Pour batter into a 9x13-inch baking pan, lined with greased foil. Bake at 350° for 30 to 33 minutes. Cool. Combine powdered sugar, butter, vanilla, and enough milk for desired consistency. Add food coloring. Remove brownie from pan and remove foil. When completely cool, frost. Cut brownie into 4 (3-inch) rows. Cut each row into seven triangles. Press chocolate pieces into frosting. Insert pretzel into one side for a tree trunk. Makes 28 trees.

101
Christmas Recipe Ideas

Candies

Coconut Macaroons

2½ c granulated sugar
2⅓ c (8 ozs) shredded,
    fresh unsweetened
    coconut
1 c egg whites
    (whites of about 6
    extra-large eggs)

1 tsp vanilla extract
⅓ c plus 2 tbsp
all-purpose flour
baker's parchment
    paper

Preheat oven to 350°. Butter a cookie sheet and cover with parchment paper. Mix sugar, coconut, and egg whites in the top of a double boiler and stir over boiling water until mixture reaches 170° on a candy thermometer. Remove from heat, and stir in vanilla and flour. Using a pastry bag with no nozzle, pipe macaroons about 1½ inches in diameter onto parchment paper. If you have no pastry bag, two teaspoons may be used. Bake for 15 minutes or until macaroons begin to turn pale gold. Remove from parchment and cool on a rack. Macaroons will keep for several weeks in an airtight container stored in a cool place.

Toffee

1 c chopped pecans	½ c margarine or
¾ c packed brown	butter
sugar	½ c semisweet
	chocolate chips

Butter a 9x9x2-inch baking pan. Spread pecans in bottom of pan. Bring brown sugar and margarine to a boil, stirring constantly. Boil over medium heat, and continue to stir for 7 minutes. Remove from heat and immediately spread mixture over pecans in pan. Sprinkle chocolate chips over hot mixture and place cookie sheet over pan until chocolate chips are melted. Smooth melted chocolate over candy and cut into ½-inch squares while hot. Chill until firm. Yields 3 dozen candies.

• • •

*Christmas is the season for
kindling the fire of hospitality in the hall,
the genial flame of charity in the heart.*

WASHINGTON IRVING

Chocolate Truffles

6 ozs (squares) dark
   semisweet chocolate
3 tbsp unsalted butter
2 tbsp powdered sugar

3 egg yolks
1 tbsp rum flavoring
½ c finely grated
   semisweet chocolate

Melt chocolate in the top of a double boiler over boiling water. Blend in butter and sugar, and stir until sugar dissolves. Remove from heat and add egg yolks, one at a time, beating well after each addition. Stir in rum flavoring. Place in a bowl covered with waxed paper overnight, but do not chill. Shape into 1-inch-diameter balls and roll in grated chocolate. Eat after a day or two. Yields 2 dozen.

Sugar Plums

1 (24-oz) container
   pitted prunes
4 ozs whole blanched
   almonds

1 c (4 ozs)
   sweetened flaked
   coconut
¼ c sugar

Insert an almond into each prune, molding fruit around the nut to create a plum shape. Mix coconut and sugar together in a small ball and roll stuffed prunes in mixture. Store in an airtight container with waxed paper between the layers. Yields about 100.

Easy Chocolate Fudge

1 c granulated sugar
¼ c cocoa
⅓ c milk
¼ c margarine or butter
1 tbsp light
    corn syrup

1 tsp vanilla
⅓ c chopped nuts
2 to 2¼ c
    powdered sugar

Combine granulated sugar and cocoa in a 2-quart saucepan. Stir in milk, margarine, and corn syrup. Bring to a boil over medium heat, stirring frequently. Boil and stir 1 minute. Remove from heat and allow to cool without stirring until bottom of pan is lukewarm (about 45 minutes). Stir in vanilla and nuts. Mix in powdered sugar until very stiff. Press in buttered loaf pan measuring 9x5x3 inches. Chill until firm and cut into 1-inch squares. Yields 32 candies.

• • •

*The people who find
the most pleasure in Christmas are the ones who
have taken control of the celebration
and shaped it to conform to
their own wishes and values.
They know what's most important about
Christmas to them. . . .*

JO ROBINSON

Peanut Brittle

1½ tsp baking soda
1 tsp water
1 tsp vanilla
1½ c sugar
1 c water

1 c light corn syrup
3 tbsp margarine or
   butter
1 lb shelled
   unroasted peanuts

Butter 2 cookie sheets and keep warm. Mix baking soda, water, and vanilla; set aside. Combine sugar, water, and corn syrup in a 3-quart saucepan and cook over medium heat, stirring occasionally until candy thermometer reads 240°, or until small amount of syrup dropped into very cold water forms a soft ball that can be flattened when removed from the water. Add margarine and peanuts, and cook to 300°, stirring constantly, or until small amounts of mixture separate into hard, brittle threads when dropped into very cold water. Remove from heat immediately and stir in baking soda mixture. Pour half of candy mixture onto each cookie sheet and quickly spread about ¼ inch thick. Cool and break into pieces. Yields 2 pounds of candy.

Choco-Butterscotch Crisps

1 c butterscotch chips
½ c peanut butter
4 c crisped rice cereal
1 c chocolate chips

2 tbsp butter
1 tbsp water
½ c powdered
    sugar

Melt butterscotch chips and peanut butter over very low heat, stirring occasionally. Add cereal and mix well. Press half of mixture in an 8x8-inch square pan and chill. Melt chocolate chips, butter, and water in top of a double boiler and add powdered sugar. Spread over chilled mixture and press in remainder of cereal mixture. Cut and chill.

Crispy Cereal Chocolate Drops

2 c (12 ozs) butterscotch chips
1 c (6 ozs) semisweet chocolate chips
½ c salted peanuts
4 c crisp cereal (almost anything will work)

Melt butterscotch chips and chocolate chips over very low heat stirring constantly until smooth. Remove from heat. Add peanuts and cereal. Stir carefully until well coated. Drop by teaspoonfuls onto waxed paper. Chill until firm. Yields 8 dozen.

Molasses Taffy

2 c very dark molasses
1 c brown sugar,
   firmly packed, or
   granulated sugar

1 tbsp vinegar
2 tbsp unsalted
   butter

Mix molasses, sugar, and vinegar in a small but heavy saucepan and stir over low heat until sugar dissolves. Cover and boil (but do not stir) until mixture reaches 245° on a candy thermometer, or forms a firm ball when dropped into cold water. Stir in butter and simmer slowly until mixture reaches 270° on candy thermometer or crackles when dropped into cold water. Pour into a buttered pan. After taffy has cooled, rub a bland oil onto your hands and take small amounts of taffy at a time, stretching to a length of about 14 inches, folding back on itself and stretching again, until all of taffy is no longer transparent but creamy and light in color and the ends hold a shape. Pull until ½ inch in diameter and cut into small squares with a pair of oiled scissors. Cool on a rack until hardened and wrap in waxed paper. Yields about 1 pound.

CRANBERRY FUDGE

4 c granulated sugar
¼ c unsalted butter
⅔ c milk
1 tbsp golden (corn)
    syrup

1 can (7 ozs)
    full-cream
    condensed milk
¾ c fresh
    cranberries

Mix sugar, butter, milk, and corn syrup in a heavy saucepan and bring slowly to a boil, stirring constantly. Add condensed milk and return to a boil for 20 minutes, while continuing to stir, until mixture reaches 250° or when a small amount dropped into very cold water sets hard. Remove from heat and stir in cranberries. Spread in well-greased jelly roll pan and cut into squares just before fudge hardens. When completely cooled, cut into pieces and store in airtight container. Yields 2 pounds of candy.

• • •

For unto us a child is born,
unto us a son is given. . .
and his name shall be called Wonderful.

ISAIAH 9:6

Popcorn Balls

½ c sugar
½ c light corn syrup
½ c margarine or butter

½ tsp salt
a few drops food color
8 c popped corn

Simmer sugar, corn syrup, margarine, salt, and food color in a 4-quart Dutch oven over medium-high heat, stirring constantly. Add popped corn and cook about 3 minutes, stirring constantly until popcorn is well coated. Cool slightly. After dipping hands into cold water, shape mixture into 2½-inch balls. Place on waxed paper and when cooled, wrap individually in plastic wrap. Makes 8 or 9 popcorn balls.

Peanut Butter Bonbons

1½ c powdered sugar
1 c graham cracker
    crumbs (about 12 squares)
½ c margarine or butter
1 tbsp shortening

½ c peanut butter
1 pkg (6 ozs)
    semisweet
    chocolate chips

Combine powdered sugar and cracker crumbs. Melt margarine and peanut butter over low heat and stir into crumb mixture. Shape into 1-inch balls. Melt chocolate chips with shortening and dip balls into chocolate with tongs until coated. Place on waxed paper and chill until firm. Yields 3 dozen candies.

Inspirational Library

Beautiful purse/pocket-size editions of Christian classics bound in flexible leatherette. These books make thoughtful gifts for everyone on your list, including yourself!

When I'm on My Knees   The highly popular collection of devotional thoughts on prayer, especially for women.
Flexible Leatherette $4.97

The Bible Promise Book   Over 1,000 promises from God's Word arranged by topic. What does God promise about matters like: Anger, Illness, Jealousy, Love, Money, Old Age, and Mercy? Find out in this book!
Flexible Leatherette $3.97

Daily Wisdom for Women   A daily devotional for women seeking biblical wisdom to apply to their lives. Scripture taken from the New American Standard Version of the Bible.
Flexible Leatherette $4.97

My Daily Prayer Journal   Each page is dated and features a Scripture verse and ample room for you to record your thoughts, prayers, and praises. One page for each day of the year.
Flexible Leatherette $4.97